ANGER MANAGEMENT

A Step By Step Instruction Handbook on How To Control and Manipulate Excessive Anger In A Healthy and Safe Way

CALOS JACK
Copyright@2018

COPYRIGHT

No part of this publication may be reproduced, distributed, or transmitted in any form or by any means, including photocopying, recording, or other electronic or mechanical methods, or by any information storage and retrieval system without the prior written permission of the publisher, except in the case of very brief quotations embodied in critical reviews and certain other non-commercial uses per-mitted by copyright law

TABLE OF CONTENT

CHAPTER 1

INTRODUCTION

Anger Management is a way or procedure which helps in controlling temper and also to improving ones skills to use anger in a positive way. It is also aimed at detecting the influence of anger and aids a clearer view on how to analyze and correct issues surrounding it.

However, this book is of great importance for anyone who needs help to managing his or her anger and frustration at workplace or other environment. It is also importance to note that before you can master any recommendation in

this book, you are expected to free your mind off any distractions and have a calm head.

CHAPTER 2

BREAKDOWN OF ANGER

Anger can be referred to as a reaction when someone feels threaten and this often begins with discomfort and eventually leads to irritation. Meanwhile, Mood swing, Hostility and Aggression are often placed for anger even as there is a little difference that distinguishes each of them from the other.

   a. Mood Swing is an emotional feeling or state that has been hanging around, which can begin from irritation and gradually to a violent expression of an individual. This kind of feelings or state of mind can sweep over other feeling or emotions that might have been there before.

b. Hostility can be a feeling of hatred, there aiding individual interpretation and assessment or judgement of situations. All these are as a result o anger in various ways.

c. Aggression is an expression of the ability to do harm to others. These kinds of feelings often leave a boiling anger inside the individual who displays such.

Short Story to Explain the Effects of Anger

Dave who lives with his wife had a quarrel in the morning, he obviously felt discomfort at his wife starting a fight that morning, in just few seconds, anger began to brew in him.

His daughter walked up to him that morning to play with her father before going to work, but Dave suddenly yells at her and this made his daughter to shed tears and eventually Dave was touched. This will certainly spoil his day because his colleagues will definitely know that Dave is not in a good mood this morning.

CHAPTER 3

BELIEFS AND LOGIC OF ANGER

All over the world today, there are different myths and beliefs about anger, some o which are not so true. Below are the few analyzed beliefs and logical conclusions.

1. Anger Management is teaches about how you can overpower anger.

Logical Conclusion: Anger Management teaches you that anger is not to be overpowered or vented out, rather, it should be expressed in a manner that does not show violent and a civilized and positive way.

2. Letting out my anger makes me relax. Withholding it is not a healthy ideal.

Logical Conclusion: It is okay to vent out your anger but it should be done in a non-aggressive manner, as it can lead to more Hostility.

3. I find it difficult to control my anger

Logical Conclusion: Like every other emotional feelings, anger in same way, is a product of the situation you may find yourself in, all that needs to be done is examine the situation before you from several points of view, keep away from oversight and walk pass the anger.

4. I secure respect, obedience and attention when i display an aggressive behaviour.

When you intimidate people aggressively, you do not ear their respect or submission. You can get their respect and submission if you try to understand them and tolerate their opinion.

CHAPTER 4

REASONS FOR ANGER MANAGEMENT

An extreme anger can affect different aspect of our lives; it includes our personal life, social life, career and our health. Anger has lead to many breakups in relationships, broken homes and even losing trust of our friends. There are some reasons why anger management is important, they are;

1. An extreme anger makes people to feel uncomfortable to socialize with you and this can be very bad when children who must have notice your anger began to stay away from you. Thus, we can say that anger affects your personal life.

2. When someone is anger, he or she easily jumps into hasty conclusion and can lead you into falsification of truth, thereby affecting your way of thinking.

3. If you cannot control your anger at your of work, due to inability to withstand critics or other opinion, your may find it difficult to have colleagues around you. This can affect your career!

4. People with a High Blood Pressure often face threat or risk when they are angry, your health should be of importance to you, and if it is, then anger management is good for you.

CHAPTER 5

POSSIBLE SYMPTOMS OF ANGER

There are symptoms of anger often caused by some factor like frustrations and unforeseen situations. These symptoms can be classified into 2 category, there are;

1. Physical

2. Mental.

Physical Symptoms: These are symptoms that may occur on the physical parts of the body when anger arose. Some of these signs are Fast Heart Beating, Sweat Buds and Muscle Stiffness.

Mental Symptoms: These type of symptoms occurs within an individual, they are Restlessness or anxiety, Discomfort and Irritation.

However, it could be more serious when the physical and mental symptoms meets, and these can lead straight to causing;

1. Crying or shedding tears

2. Throwing of objects

3. Banging of doors

4. Punching of walls

5. Screaming

6. Arguments

It is pivotal to note that it is the way you react to people who aims at making you angry that gets you angry.

CHAPTER 6

NAGETIVE EMOTIONS

Anger as an emotion is being triggered by other negative emotions, and if it is not handled with care, it can go beyond your control and this get the whole body alert for fight or a serious aggressive and violent behaviour.

The negative emotions that can lead to anger include;

1. Blames: when you begin to blame people for certain issues rather than looking deep into yourself to point out the problem can lead to anger.

2. Rigid Mind Set: This is when you do not accept other people's opinion, force them to agree to yours and have a non-bargained opinion.

3. Jumping into Conclusions: This is when you assume what other people

might be doing or getting at without hearing from them.

4. Thinking Hard: This is when you begin to have hard thoughts on yourself, for example, Nobody want to know how am doing, why am I experiencing this?, everybody hates me.

CHAPTER 7

STAGE OF ANGER

Anger begins at a particular stage and later grows into another stage, either gradually or precipitously. There are 3 stages of anger or aggression, they are;

1. Escalation Stage: Here in this stage, you begin to experience signs given out by your body when the anger is brewing. The signs include the mental and physical signs.

2. Expression Stage: When you have ignored or refused to pay attention to

the signs that appear in the Escalation stage, it can develop into the next stage, thereby, getting to a violent aggressive behaviour, which can be physical or verbal.

3. Post-Expression Stage: This is the last stage of anger, it involves understand the negative consequences of the actions taken as a result of anger, it could be feelings

of guilt, shame, remorse and even to other outward consequences like being apprehended or arrested.

Duration of anger from one stage to another varies from one individual to another. Some may get to the third stage in a matter of seconds or minutes, while some may take a longer time to cross a Escalation stage. The objective of Anger Management is to keep you away from getting to the Expression stage of anger and can help you not to get to the Escalation stage through an effective practice.

CHAPTER 8

ALBERT ELLIS A-B-C-D MODEL

Albert Ellis developed the A-B-C-D model and today, it is recognised as one of the most potent therapy to worn down anger. The A-B-C-D model means the following

"A"... means *Activating Agent*: The incident that generates anger.

"B"...means *Belief:* This is how you understand the activating agent.

"C"... means **_Consequence_**: It is the way you feel or act in response to your belief.

"D"... means **_Dispute_**: This is a pivotal aspect of anger management; it simply means checking the belief, if they are true or a mere hallucination.

Explanation...

A- Activating Agent

You were walking down the street, someone drove his car and splashes water on you and drove off without saying sorry.

B- Belief

Your thoughts: Everyone driving is reckless, because you do not own a car.

C- Consequence

Your heart is beating fast and your muscle are stiff, you feel like you want to insult every person driving a car pass you.

D- Dispute

You can easily say to yourself: Maybe he did notice he had splashed water on me.

CHAPTER 9

HOW TO MANIPULATE ANGER

Anger is something we can control or manipulated, its gravity can be reduced if you apply the suggestions below.

1. Understand your feelings: For one to control or manipulate anger, you need to understand or differentiate feelings of remorse,, insecurity, shame and embarrassment.

2. Controlling Signs and Causes: By controlling what makes you angry,

you can also control the signs that show that you are anger. Remember that anger energises the violent part of the mind.

3. Knowing your Anger Buttons: This involves you know when you are getting angry by noticing yourself doing the following

   a. Heavy breathing

   b. Pacing round the house

   c. Redness of the face

   d. Clenching of jaw

e. Heart beating fast

4. Learning new ways to calm down:
You can control your anger faster by
learning new ways to calm down.
This ways include; taking a deep
breath, doing exercise, listening to
good music, counting to 20 slowly.

5. Express your anger in a healthier
way: Anger can sometimes become a
motivation, if you put it through the
right track. A good example is an

athlete making use of anger to perform wonderfully well.

6. Taking a minute to think about the issue: Think of how the issue can help or

Mar you day and if it is worth it can be of a great help to controlling your anger.

CHAPTER 10

IMPROVE ON YOURSELF

It is very helpful when you improve on yourself, your communications and interpretations of short or long term belief. You can do this by;

1. Becoming a good Listener: you should learn how to listen to what others have to say, rather than being the first to speak.

2. Expressing your true feelings: This is where you should express that feeling

that drives you angry, it can be shame, remorse, frustration or fright.

3. Avoid Mind Reading: This will give you a calmness that you can ever imagine, and do not jump into conclusions so quick.

4. Keep Calm: Do not fight back immediately, try finding out the true feelings the other person's anger.

CHAPTER 11

TIPS TO GO WITH

Below are few tips you should know to help in your anger management.

1. Take a deep breath: practice and master how to take a deep breath anything you are getting angry.

2. Think before you Speak: gather your thoughts within you before saying anything out.

3. Sense of humour: you can make use of humour to calm situations, rather than turning it into violence.

4. Think of possible solutions: It is better to sort for solutions to problem or situations, rather than having thoughts of what and who makes you angry.

5. Exercise: Doing exercise helps to release tension from the body, engage in any exercise you enjoy the most.

6. Display anger peacefully: you should say your thoughts out for people to hear you out, rather than turning violent to hurt others.

7. Take some time to relax: taking time to relax can help a lot, keep quiet and stay focus on your thoughts.

8. Discard grudges: When we forgive and forget anyone who offends us, it can take out a whole lot of negative emotions from us.

9. Make use of "I" statement: you can say, "I'm still expecting to see what you can offer, instead of, You don't have anything to offer in this company"

10.   Go for counselling: You can request or seek a professional assistance when you think your anger is not controllable.

THE END